LOVE

LOVE

QUOTES AND PASSAGES
FROM THE HEART

EDITED BY B.C. ARONSON

RANDOM HOUSE REFERENCE

NEW YORK TORONTO LONDON SYDNEY AUCKLAND

Please address inquiries about electronic licensing of any products for use on a network, in software, or on CD-ROM to the Subsidiary Rights Department, Random House Information Group, fax 212-572-6003.

This book is available at special discounts for bulk purchases for sales promotions or premiums. Special editions, including personalized covers, excerpts of existing books, and corporate imprints, can be created in large quantities for special needs. For more information, write to Random House, Inc., Special Markets/Premium Sales, 1745 Broadway, MD 6-2, New York, NY 10019 or e-mail specialmarkets@randomhouse.com.

Visit the Random House Reference Web site: www.randomwords.com

Library of Congress Cataloging-in-Publication Data

Love : quotes and passages from the heart / edited by B.C. Aronson.

   p. cm.

  ISBN-13: 978-0-375-72216-5 (alk. paper)

  1. Love—Quotations, maxims, etc.   I. Aronson, B. C.

PN6084.L6L665 2007

302.3—dc22   2006048720

Printed in the United States of America

10 9 8 7 6 5

ISBN: 978-0-375-72216-5

For my mother,
Barbara Anne Whitney Burch

"THE ANGELS ... SINGING UNTO ONE ANOTHER,
CAN FIND AMONG THEIR BURNING TERMS OF LOVE,
NONE SO DEVOTIONAL AS THAT OF "MOTHER"

—EDGAR ALLAN POE

Contents

Introduction

The novelist and poet Margaret Atwood wrote, "The Eskimo has fifty-two names for snow because it is important to them; there ought to be as many for love." If you were to ask a young boy, his mother, his teenage sister, and his grandfather, "What does love mean to you?" you would no doubt receive four quite different responses. Ask fifty-two people and you'll probably get fifty-two different definitions. A new mother will more than likely describe the love between herself and her child. Newlyweds could point to their own thrilling companionship. A man with grown children who have their own kids might bring up the web of love of a large family. An older gentleman who never married would be justified in mentioning his love of a great steak dinner with all the trimmings. The variations are endless.

So it is that, in compiling a book of quotations about love, there is a vast well of material from which to draw. Whole volumes could be put together from William Shakespeare's sonnets and plays alone. Romantic novels from ages past to the present day extol the virtues of love and present more sources. So do song lyrics from the fifties, say. And the works of Plato, Bill Cosby, Woody Allen, and anyone who has ever written about spiritual life, friendship, cats, dogs, and almost anything else you can think of. Love really is all around.

Personally, I am grateful for the love of my husband. For close to thirty years of marriage, he has always been there for me, no matter what. He patiently went along with my crazy idea of renewing our twenty-fifth wedding anniversary vows at a Las Vegas wedding chapel with an Elvis impersonator/justice of the peace presiding. As he is neither an Elvis fan nor a fan of Las Vegas kitsch, this little event wasn't something he would have chosen for himself. But he came through it all relatively unscathed. Then, as we were flying home, he told me he'd had a delightful time after all. It was confirmed for me again: he's my partner for life.

I am also most thankful for my "family of choice,"

otherwise known as my friends. They are a small but diverse bunch; each and every one is very special to me (and to my husband as well). Through good times and bad, they have stood by me with their love and support and done so without complaint. Not a day goes by that I don't thank the Good Lord above for the gift of their friendship. I kept my personal experiences in mind as I was looking for material for this book.

To keep *Love* manageable, it doesn't have fifty-two separate chapters of quotes. Rather, there are eleven sections, ranging from family love to true love, not that these represent the two opposite ends of the spectrum of love, you understand. There are no walls between these chapters—the same love often belongs in many sections. I offer the following sayings in the hope that something will resonate with the way you're feeling right now and that somehow, in whatever way, your life is touched with love.

ONE:

Family

IT ALL BEGINS WITH A FAMILY. THE FIRST LOVE WE FEEL IS FROM OUR MOTHER EVEN AS SHE CARRIES US. A FAMILY GROWS AROUND THAT LOVE IN AS MANY COMBINATIONS AS THERE ARE INDIVIDUALS: FROM THE FIRST, A FATHER, THEN BROTHERS AND SISTERS PERHAPS; GRANDPARENTS, UNCLES, AUNTS, AND COUSINS; AND MAYBE EVEN OUR OWN SONS AND DAUGHTERS DOWN THE ROAD. A BIG BROTHER STANDING UP TO A BULLY, A SISTER PUTTING ON YOUR MAKEUP, GRANDPARENTS SPOILING THE KIDS ROTTEN. THE LOVE WE GET FROM OUR FAMILY IS OUR ROCK.

A mother's love for her child is like nothing
else in the world. It knows no law, no pity,
it dares all things and crushes down
remorselessly all that stands in its path.

—*Agatha Christie, writer*

Mother love has been much maligned. An over
mothered boy may go through life expecting
each new woman to love him the way his mother
did. Her love may make any other love seem
inadequate. But an unloved boy would be
even more likely to idealize love. I don't
think it's possible for a mother or father
to love a child too much.

—*Frank Pittman, psychiatrist and family therapist*

Unconditional love is loving your kids
for who they are, not for what they do . . . it
isn't something you will achieve every
minute of every day. But it is the thought
we must hold in our hearts every day.
—*Stephanie Marston, family therapist and writer*

The most important thing a father can do
for his children is to love their mother.
—*Henry Ward Beecher, preacher*

Where does the family start? It starts with a
young man falling in love with a girl—no
superior alternative has yet been found.
—*Winston Churchill, political leader*

Of course if you like your kids, if you love them from the moment they begin, you yourself begin all over again, in them and with them.

—*William Saroyan, writer*

You can see them alongside the shuffleboard courts in Florida or on the porches of the old folks' homes up north. . . . They are in love, they have always been in love, although sometimes they would have denied it. And because they have been in love they have survived everything that life could throw at them, even their own failures.

—*Ernest Havemann, writer*

In family life, love is the oil that eases friction,
the cement that binds closer together,
and the music that brings harmony.
—*Eva Burrows, Salvation Army general*

Family love is messy, clinging,
and of an annoying and repetitive
pattern, like bad wallpaper.
—*Friedrich Nietzsche, philosopher*

In truth a family is what you make it. It is made strong, not by number of heads counted at the dinner table, but by the rituals you help family members create, by the memories you share, by the commitment of time, caring, and love you show to one another, and by the hopes for the future you have as individuals and as a unit.

—Marge Kennedy, writer, and
Janet Spencer King, writer

[A mother] discovers with great delight that one does not love one's children just because they are one's children but because of the friendship formed while raising them.

—Gabriel García Márquez, writer

6

The Family is the Country of the heart.
There is an angel in the Family who, by the
mysterious influence of grace, of sweetness, and
of love, renders the fulfillment of duties less
wearisome, sorrows less bitter. The only
pure joys unmixed with sadness.

—*Giuseppe Mazzini, Italian politician*

Smile at each other, smile at your wife,
smile at your husband, smile at your children,
smile at each other—it doesn't matter who it is—
and that will help you to grow up
in greater love for each other.

—*Mother Teresa, humanitarian*

No man has ever lived that had enough
of children's gratitude or woman's love.

—*William Butler Yeats, poet*

⚮

I take my children everywhere,
but they always find their way back home.

—*Robert Orben, magician*

⚮

Happiness is having a large, loving, caring,
close-knit family in another city.

—*George Burns, actor*

The real question isn't
whether or not you love your kids,
but how well you are able
to demonstrate your love and
caring so that your children
really feel loved.

—STEPHANIE MARSTON,
family therapist and writer

The last step in parental love
involves the release of the beloved;
the willing cutting of the cord that
would otherwise keep the child in a
state of emotional dependence.

—*Lewis Mumford, social critic and writer*

So if you have a grandma, Thank
the Good Lord up above, And give
Grandmama hugs and kisses,
For grandmothers are to love.

—*Lois Wyse, writer*

Oh, I love to see a man with a cigar. It reminds
me of my grandfather. Morning to night,
he used to sit with a great big stogie dangling
from his lips. Oh, the hours we kids used
to spend sitting on his lap, playing with the
yellow whiskers beneath his nose. Then he'd
take out his teeth with the cigar still in them
and chase us around the room! We'd all laugh
and laugh . . . then suddenly Grampa's mood
would change, and we'd all have to run for our
lives. . . . You can't buy memories like that.

—*Daphne,* Frasier

Children begin by loving their parents.
After a time they judge them. Rarely,
if ever, do they forgive them.

—*Oscar Wilde, playwright and writer*

It is my pleasure that my children are free
and happy, and unrestrained by parental tyranny.
Love is the chain whereby to bind a child
to its parents.

—*Abraham Lincoln, U.S. President*

∽∾

Perfect love sometimes does not come
until the first grandchild.

—*Welsh proverb*

∽∾

The reason grandparents and grandchildren get
along so well is that they have a common enemy.

—*Sam Levenson, humorist*

We never know

THE LOVE OF OUR PARENTS

FOR US TILL WE HAVE

BECOME PARENTS.

—HENRY WARD BEECHER,
PREACHER

two:

Friends

ONE OF THE GREAT TRUTHS OF LIFE
IS THAT WHILE YOU'RE STUCK WITH YOUR
FAMILY, YOU CAN CHOSE YOUR FRIENDS.
THERE IS A DIFFERENT LOVE THAT FLESH
AND BLOOD CANNOT GUARANTEE: THE LOVE
OF A FRIEND WHO KNOWS YOU, DOESN'T JUDGE
YOU, AND WILL BE THERE FOR YOU
NO MATTER WHAT. TRUE FRIENDS
ARE NEVER *JUST* FRIENDS.

To have a good friend is the purest
of all God's gifts, for it is a love
that has no exchange of payment.
It is not inherited, as with a family.
It is not compelling, as with a child.
And it has no means of physical
pleasure, as with a mate. It is,
therefore, an indescribable bond
that brings with it a far deeper
devotion than all the others.

—FRANCES FARMER, ACTRESS

A friend is one who knows you
and loves you just the same.
—*Elbert Hubbard, writer and publisher*

The best mirror is an old friend.
—*George Herbert, poet*

The friend who holds your hand and says
the wrong thing is made of dearer stuff
than the one who stays away.
—*Barbara Kingsolver, writer*

All you'll get from strangers is surface
pleasantry or indifference. Only someone
who loves you will criticize you.

—Judith Crist, film critic

❧

Friendship is the perfection of love,
and superior to love; it is love purified,
exalted, proved by experience and a
consent of minds. Love, Madam, may, and
love does, often stop short of friendship.

—Samuel Richardson, writer

❧

With true friends . . . even water
drunk together is sweet enough.

—Chinese proverb

Greater love has no man than this, that a man
lay down his life for his friends.

—*John 15:13*

If there ever comes a day when
we can't be together, keep me in your heart,
I'll stay there forever.

—*A. A. Milne, writer,* Winnie the Pooh

Can miles truly separate you from friends. . . . If
you want to be with someone you love,
aren't you already there?

—*Richard Bach, writer*

Friendship is certainly the finest balm
for the pangs of disappointed love.

—*Jane Austen, writer*

Sympathy constitutes friendship; but in love
there is a sort of antipathy, or opposing passion.
Each strives to be the other, and both
together make up one whole.

—*Samuel Taylor Coleridge, poet*

There's nothing worth the wear of winning
but laughter, and the love of friends.

—*Hilaire Belloc, writer*

Friendship marks a life even more deeply than
love. Love risks degenerating into obsession,
friendship is never anything but sharing.
—*Elie Wiesel, Holocaust survivor and writer*

All love that has not friendship for its base,
is like a mansion built upon the sand.
—*Ella Wheeler Wilcox, poet*

Platonic Love is a fool's name for the affection
between a disability and a frost.
—*Ambrose Bierce, writer*

Platonic love is love from the neck up.

—*Thyra Samter Winslow, writer*

Friendship is love minus sex and plus reason.
Love is friendship plus sex and minus reason.

—*Mason Cooley, aphorist*

Love is blind; friendship closes its eyes.

—*Anonymous*

Friendship is Love without his wings!

—*Lord Byron, poet*

Friendship is a serious affection; the most sublime of all affections, because it is founded on principle, and cemented by time. The very reverse may be said of love. In a great degree, love and friendship cannot subsist in the same bosom; even when inspired by different objects they weaken or destroy each other, and for the same object can only be felt in succession. The vain fears and fond jealousies, the winds which fan the flame of love, when judiciously or artfully tempered, are both incompatible with the tender confidence and sincere respect of friendship.

—*Mary Wollstonecraft, writer*

$\mathcal{G}$et a life in which you are not
alone. Find people you love, and
who love you. And remember that
love is not leisure, it is work.

—ANNA QUINDLEN, WRITER

Accountability in friendship is
the equivalent of love without strategy.
—*Anita Brookner, writer and art historian*

Between men and women there
is no friendship possible. There is passion,
enmity, worship, love, but no friendship.
—*Oscar Wilde, playwright and writer*

What men call friendship is no more
than a partnership, a mutual care of interests,
an exchange of favors—in a word, it is a sort
of traffic, in which self-love ever proposes
to be the gainer.
—*François de la Rochefoucauld, writer and moralist*

The more we love our friends, the less
we flatter them; it is by excusing nothing
that pure love shows itself.

—*Molière, playwright*

⁂

So long as we love we serve;
so long as we are loved by others,
I would almost say that we are indispensable;
and no man is useless while he has a friend.

—*Robert Louis Stevenson, writer*

Friendship often ends in love;
but love in friendship—never.
—*Charles Caleb Colton,*
clergyman and writer

⧼⧽

When we hurt each other we should write it
down in the sand, so the winds of forgiveness
can make it go away for good. When we help
each other we should chisel it in stone, lest
we never forget the love of a friend.
—*Christian H. Godefroy, writer*

Winning has always meant much to me,
but winning friends has meant the most.
—*Babe Didrikson Zaharias, athlete*

Friends show their love—in times
of trouble, not in happiness.
—*Euripides, playwright*

Life is to be fortified by many
friendships. To love and to be loved is
the greatest happiness of existence.
—*Sydney Smith, clergyman and writer*

tHRee:

Beginnings

FOR SOME PEOPLE, FALLING IN LOVE
IS A PHYSICAL SENSATION — IT'S IMPLIED
BY THE PHRASE: WE'RE FALLING AND WE'RE
GOING TO FEEL SOMETHING AS WE HIT THE
DECK. EVEN THOUGH IT'S THE SUSTAINED
EFFORT THAT TAKES THE PLACE OF THAT
INITIAL MADNESS THAT MAKES LOVE LAST,
WE STILL HOLD ON TO THAT NEW-LOVE
FEELING AS LONG AS WE CAN.

A youth with his first cigar makes himself sick;
a youth with his first girl makes everybody sick.

—*Mary Wilson Little, writer*

Love at first sight is easy to understand;
it's when two people have been looking
at each other for a lifetime that
it becomes a miracle.

—*Sam Levenson, humorist*

Love is what happens to men and
women who don't know each other.

—*W. Somerset Maugham, writer*

To love deeply in one direction
makes us more loving in all others.
—*Anne-Sophie Swetchine, hostess*

No, this trick won't work. . . . How on earth
are you ever going to explain in terms
of chemistry and physics so important
a biological phenomenon as first love?
—*Albert Einstein, physicist*

Love is the flower of life, and blossoms
unexpectedly and without law, and must be
plucked where it is found, and enjoyed
for the brief hour of its duration.
—*D. H. Lawrence, writer*

First love is a kind of vaccination
which saves a man from catching
the complaint the second time.

—*Honoré de Balzac, writer*

＊

At the touch of love, everyone becomes a poet.

—*Plato, philosopher*

＊

Love is like quicksilver in the hand.
Leave the fingers open and it stays.
Clutch it, and it darts away.

—*Dorothy Parker, writer*

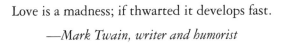

Love is a madness; if thwarted it develops fast.

—*Mark Twain, writer and humorist*

Love is like war, easy to begin but hard to end.

—*Anonymous*

Falling in love consists merely in uncorking the imagination and bottling the common-sense.

—*Helen Rowland, humorist*

I have learned not to worry about love; but to honor its coming with all my heart.

—*Alice Walker, writer*

I believe in love, but I don't
sit around waiting for it.
—*Renee Zellweger, actor*

What is irritating about love is
that it is a crime that requires an accomplice.
—*Charles Baudelaire, writer and critic*

I cannot fix on the hour, or the spot, or the
look, or the words, which laid the foundation.
It is too long ago. I was in the middle
before I knew that I had begun.
—*Fitzwilliam Darcy {on his love for Elizabeth
Bennett}, in* Pride and Prejudice

Many people when they fall in love look
for a little haven of refuge from the world,
where they can be sure of being admired
when they are not admirable, and praised
when they are not praiseworthy.

—*Bertrand Russell, mathematician and philosopher*

The art of love . . . is largely the art of persistence.

—*Albert Ellis, psychotherapist*

It is an extra dividend when you like
the girl you've fallen in love with.

—*Clark Gable, actor*

You can't buy love, but you can pay heavily for it.

—*Henny Youngman, comedian*

How delicious is the winning
of a kiss at love's beginning.

—*Thomas Campbell, poet*

Love is a deep well from which you may drink
often, but into which you may fall but once.

—*Ellye Howell Glover, writer*

We don't believe in rheumatism
and true love until after the first attack.

—*Marie von Ebner-Eschenbach, writer*

Sweet Love of youth, forgive if I forget thee,

While the world's tide is bearing me along:

Sterner desires and other hopes beset me,

Hopes which obscure, but cannot do thee wrong!

—emily brontë, writer

I was nauseous and tingly all over.
I was either in love or I had smallpox.

—*Woody Allen, director and writer*

Love is like an hourglass, with the heart
filling up as the brain empties.

—*Jule Renard, writer*

Gravitation cannot be held responsible
for people falling in love.

—*Albert Einstein, physicist*

Love doesn't just sit there, like a stone;
it has to be made, like bread,
remade all the time, made new.

—*Ursula K. Le Guin, writer*

Man reaches the highest point
of lovableness at 12 to 17—to get it back,
in a second flowering, at the age of 70 to 90.

—*Isak Dinesen, writer*

Love is a smoke raised with the fume of sighs;
Being purged, a fire sparkling in lovers' eyes;
Being vex'd a sea nourish'd with lovers' tears:
    What is it else? a madness most discreet,
    A choking gall and a preserving sweet.
        —*Romeo in William Shakespeare's*
        Romeo and Juliet

four:

Companionship

BOOKS UPON BOOKS COULD BE FILLED
WITH VARIATIONS ON AMBROSE BIERCE'S
APHORISM ON LOVE, THAT IT IS
"A TEMPORARY INSANITY, CURABLE
BY MARRIAGE." LOVE IS NOT ANTITHETICAL
TO MARRIAGE, OF COURSE. MARRIAGE ITSELF
IS A LEGAL ENTITY; THE COMPANIONSHIP
OF TWO PEOPLE IS INFINITELY MORE THAN
A PIECE OF PAPER, IT'S A STATE OF MIND,
A CHALLENGE, A COMMITMENT,
ALL DEFINED BY LOVE.

If you want to read about love and marriage
you've got to buy two separate books.

—*Alan King, comedian*

When you are in love with someone you want
to be near him all the time, except when you are
out buying things and charging them to him.

—*Miss Piggy, Muppet*

A happy marriage is a long conversation
which always seems too short.

—*André Maurois, writer*

*W*e are not the same persons this year as last; nor are those we love. It is a happy chance if we, changing, continue to love a changed person.

—W. SOMERSET MAUGHAM, WRITER

The first duty of love is to listen.

—*Paul Tillich, theologian*

You don't marry someone you can
live with—you marry the person
who you cannot live without.

—*Anonymous*

Behind every successful man
is a surprised woman!

—*Maryon Pearson, wife of
the Canadian prime minister,
Lester Pearson*

Love is an act of endless forgiveness,
a tender look which becomes a habit.

—*Peter Ustinov, actor*

My most brilliant achievement was my ability
to be able to persuade my wife to marry me.

—*Winston Churchill, political leader*

Sexiness wears thin after a while and beauty
fades, but to be married to a man who makes
you laugh every day, ah, now that's a real treat.

—*Joanne Woodward, actor and director*

Marriage is not a ritual or an end.
It is a long, intricate, intimate dance together
and nothing matters more than your own sense
of balance and your choice of partner.

—*Amy Bloom, psychotherapist and writer*

Love does not consist in gazing at
each other, but in looking outward
together in the same direction.

—*Antoine de Saint-Exupéry, writer*

Love is composed of a single soul
inhabiting two bodies.

—*Aristotle, philosopher*

I married the first man I ever kissed. When I tell
this to my children, they just about throw up.

—*Barbara Bush, former first lady*

Love: Two minds without a single thought.

—*Philip Barry, playwright*

Tenderness emerges from the fact that
the two persons, longing, as all individuals do,
to overcome the separateness and isolation
to which we are all heir because
we are individuals, can participate
in a relationship that, for the moment,
is not of two isolated selves but a union.

—*Rollo May, philosopher*

I recently read that love is entirely
a matter of chemistry. That must be why
my wife treats me like toxic waste.

—David Bissonette, writer

You can't put a price tag on love,
but you can on all its accessories.

—Melanie Clark, writer

When you love someone,
all your saved-up wishes start coming out.

—Elizabeth Bowen, writer

No man is truly married until he understands
every word his wife is NOT saying.

—*Anonymous*

To get the full value of joy you must
have someone to divide it with.

—*Mark Twain, writer and humorist*

"The whole world loves a lover" is an interesting
theory, but a very bad legal defense.

—*Keith Sullivan, writer*

I was married by a judge.
I should have asked for a jury.

—*Groucho Marx, actor and comedian*

❦

They say love is blind . . . and marriage is an
institution. Well, I'm not ready for an
institution for the blind just yet.

—*Mae West, actor*

❦

I think men who have a pierced ear
are better prepared for marriage. They've
experienced pain and bought jewelry.

—*Rita Rudner, comedian*

A woman can forgive a man for the harm
he does her . . . but she can never forgive him
for the sacrifices he makes on her account.

—*W. Somerset Maugham, writer*

An archaeologist is the best husband
a woman can have; the older she gets,
the more interested he is in her.

—*Agatha Christie, writer*

So heavy is the chain of wedlock that it needs
two to carry it, and sometimes three.

—*Alexandre Dumas, dramatist and writer*

In olden times sacrifices were made at the altar,
a custom which is still continued.

—*Helen Rowland, humorist*

Keep your eyes wide open before marriage,
half shut afterwards.

—*Benjamin Franklin, statesman*

In the race for love, I was scratched.

—*Joan Davis, actor*

Marriage has no guarantees. If that's what you're
looking for, go live with a car battery.

—*Erma Bombeck, columnist*

To keep the fire burning brightly there's one
easy rule: Keep the two logs together, near
enough to keep each other warm and far enough
apart—about a finger's breadth—for breathing
room. Good fire, good marriage, same rule.

—*Marnie Reed Crowell, writer*

Look for a sweet person. Forget rich.

—*Estée Lauder, entrepreneur*

Love seems the swiftest but it is the slowest
of all growths. No man or woman
really knows what perfect love is until they
have been married a quarter of a century.

—*Mark Twain, writer and humorist*

One of the silliest lines ever said in
a feature film came from *Love Story*, the 1970s
hit, which immortalized the phrase,
"Love means never having to say you're sorry."
There are few people who would actually
want to share a life with someone who held
that concept near and dear.

—*Marge Kennedy, writer*

True love comes quietly, without
banners or flashing lights. If you hear
bells, get your ears checked.

—*Erich Segal, writer and screenwriter*

Infatuation is when you think he's as sexy as
Robert Redford, as smart as Henry Kissinger,
as noble as Ralph Nader, as funny as Woody
Allen, and as athletic as Jimmy Conners. Love
is when you realize that he's as sexy as Woody
Allen, as smart as Jimmy Connors, as funny as
Ralph Nader, as athletic as Henry Kissinger
and nothing like Robert Redford—but
you'll take him anyway.

—*Judith Viorst, writer*

Without love, what are we worth?
Eighty-nine cents! Eighty-nine cents worth
of chemicals walking around lonely.

—*Benjamin Franklin (Hawkeye) Pierce,*
M*A*S*H

Love is the magician that pulls
man out of his own hat.

—*Ben Hecht, writer and director*

Love is like a friendship caught on fire.
In the beginning a flame, very pretty, often hot
and fierce, but still only light and flickering.
As love grows older, our hearts mature and our
love becomes as coals, deep-burning and
unquenchable.

—*Bruce Lee, actor and martial artist*

We waste time looking for the perfect lover,
instead of creating the perfect love.

—*Tom Robbins, writer*

Men love because they are afraid of themselves,
afraid of the loneliness that lives in them, and
need someone in whom they can lose themselves
as smoke loses itself in the sky.

—*V. F. Calverton, intellectual*

[W]hen you realize you want to spend the rest
of your life with somebody, you want the rest
of your life to start as soon as possible.

—*Harry Burns,* When Harry Met Sally

[Being in love] is something like poetry.
Certainly, you can analyze it and expound its
various senses and intentions, but there is always
something left over, mysteriously hovering
between music and meaning.

—*Muriel Spark, writer*

We are so fond of each other
because our ailments are the same.

—*Jonathan Swift, writer*

When I eventually met Mr. Right I had
no idea that his first name was Always.

—*Rita Rudner, comedian*

What is there in the vale of life
Half so delightful as a wife
When Friendship, love and peace combine
To stamp the marriage bond divine?
—*William Cowper, poet*

Marrying for love may be a bit risky, but it is
so honest that God can't help but smile on it.
—*Josh Billings, essayist and humorist*

Love is moral even without legal marriage,
but marriage is immoral without love.
—*Ellen Key, writer and critic*

A virtuous wife is a man's best treasure.

—*Muhammad*

A wife is the joy of a man's heart.

—*Talmud*

ED COUCH: What the hell's this?

EVELYN COUCH: That's a low cholesterol meal. Happy Valentine's.

ED COUCH: God! Are you trying to kill me?

EVELYN COUCH: If I was gonna kill you, I'd use my hands.

—*Fanny Flagg,* Fried Green Tomatoes

I thought I was in love once, and
then later I thought maybe it was
just an inner-ear imbalance.

—*Benton Fraser,* Due South

When love is strong, a man and a
woman can make their bed on a sword's blade.
When love grows weak, a bed of 60 cubits
is not large enough.

—*Talmud*

Of all the paths [that] lead to a woman's love
Pity's the straightest.

—*Francis Beaumont and John Fletcher, dramatists*

To see her is to love her,
And love but her forever;
For Nature made her what she is,
And never made another.

—*Robert Burns, poet*

⚬

We have lived and loved together
Through many changing years;
We have shared each other's gladness,
And wept each other's tears.

—*Charles Jefferys, lyricist*

⚬

Being in therapy is great. I spend
an hour just talking about myself.
It's kinda like being the guy on a date.

—*Caroline Rhea, comedian and actor*

Whenever you want to marry someone,
go have lunch with his ex-wife.

—*Shelley Winters, actor*

I sold my memoirs of my love life
to Parker Brothers and they are going
to make a game out of it.

—*Woody Allen, director and writer*

I have learned that only two things
are necessary to keep one's wife happy.
First, let her think she's having her own way.
And second, let her have it.

—*Lyndon B. Johnson, U.S. President*

Politics doesn't make strange
bedfellows—marriage does.

—*Groucho Marx, actor and comedian*

Someone asked me why women don't
gamble as much as men do, and I gave the
commonsensical reply that we don't have as
much money. That was a true and incomplete
answer. In fact, women's total instinct for
gambling is satisfied by marriage.

—*Gloria Steinem, writer*

The secret of a happy
marriage remains a secret.

—*Henny Youngman, comedian*

I've given my memoirs far more thought than
any of my marriages. You can't divorce a book.

—*Gloria Swanson, actor*

Americans, who make more of
marrying for love than any other people,
also break up more of their marriages, but
the figure reflects not so much the failure
of love as the determination of people
not to live without it.

—*Morton Hunt, writer*

The highest prize in a world of men is the
most beautiful woman available on your arm
and living there in her heart loyal to you.

—*Normal Mailer, writer*

Love is what makes two people sit
in the middle of a bench when there
is plenty of room at both ends.

—*Anonymous*

∽

A man loves his sweetheart the most,
his wife the best, but his mother the longest.

—*Irish proverb*

∽

No woman ever falls in love with a man unless
she has a better opinion of him than he deserves.

—*Edgar Watson Howe, writer*

The bravest thing that men do is love women.

—*Mort Sahl, comedian*

A woman has to love a bad man once or twice
in her life, to be thankful for a good one.

—*Marjorie Kinnan Rawlings, writer*

Love is passion, obsession, someone you can't
live without. If you don't start with that, what
are you going to end up with? Fall head
over heels. I say find someone you can love
like crazy and who'll love you the same way
back. And how do you find him? Forget
your head and listen to your heart.

—*William Parrish, politician*

One of the things my life has taught me
is how important it is to try to say, "I love you"
in ways that can be preserved, looked at,
and read when you are alone or when
there is adversity or when circumstances bring
separation. In any case, . . . saying "I love you"
is one of the "secrets" of the happy marriage that
Ronnie and I have shared. Ronnie's letters move
me to this day. They are his gift to me across
the years, and throughout the decades of love.

—*Nancy Reagan, former first lady*

The most wonderful of all things in life is the discovery of another human being with whom one's relationship has a growing depth, beauty and joy as the years increase. This inner progressiveness of love between two human beings is a most marvelous thing; it cannot be found by looking for it or by passionately wishing for it. It is a sort of divine accident, and the most wonderful of all things in life.

—HUGH WALPOLE, WRITER

five:

Passion

PASSION IS MANIFESTED IN MANY WAYS
WHEN TWO PEOPLE ARE IN LOVE. THERE
IS THE BLIND MADNESS THAT LOVE CAN CAUSE
WHEN IT IS YOUNG AND EXUBERANT (WHEN
THEY ARE "MADLY" IN LOVE). WE ALSO SEE
PASSION WHEN LOVE IS THWARTED OR
TURNED AWAY. AND PASSION IS PLAYED
OUT IN THE SEXUAL EXPRESSION OF LOVE
BETWEEN TWO PEOPLE. HERE, PASSION
CAN PREFIGURE LOVE, SUPPORT LOVE,
DESCRIBE LOVE, AND SIGNAL ITS MOST
INTIMATE ARTICULATION FOR US.

Love is of all passions the strongest,
for it attacks simultaneously the head,
the heart and the senses.

—*Lao Tzu, philosopher*

❧

Law and love are the same—
romantic in concept but the actual
practice can give you a yeast infection.

—*Ally McBeal,* Ally McBeal

In my sex fantasy, nobody
ever loves me for my mind.
—*Nora Ephron, screenwriter
and director*

∞

The human race has been set up. Someone,
somewhere, is playing a practical joke on us.
Apparently, women need to feel loved to have
sex. Men need to have sex to feel loved.
How do we ever get started?
—*Billy Connolly, actor*

∞

You call it madness, but I call it love.
—*Don Byas, musician*

Passion, it lies in all of us, sleeping . . .
waiting . . . and though unwanted . . .
unbidden . . . it will stir . . . open its jaws and
howl. It speaks to us . . . guides us . . . passion
rules us all, and we obey. What other choice
do we have? Passion is the source of our finest
moments. The joy of love . . . the clarity
of hatred . . . and the ecstasy of grief. It hurts
sometimes more than we can bear. If we could
live without passion maybe we'd know some
kind of peace . . . but we would be hollow. . . .
Empty rooms shuttered and dank. Without
passion we'd be truly dead.

—*Joss Whedon, writer and director*

There is always

SOME MADNESS IN LOVE.

BUT THERE IS ALSO ALWAYS

SOME REASON IN MADNESS.

—FRIEDRICH NIETZSCHE, PHILOSOPHER

Passion makes the world go round.
Love just makes it a safer place.

—*Ice T, rapper and actor*

Love is an exploding cigar we willingly smoke.

—*Lynda Barry, cartoonist*

Love is not altogether a delirium, yet it has
many points in common therewith.

—*Thomas Carlyle, historian*

Love is an irresistible desire
to be irresistibly desired.

—*Robert Frost, poet*

Q&O

A kiss is a lovely trick designed by nature
to stop speech when words become superfluous.

—*Ingrid Bergman, actor*

Q&O

Soul meets soul on lover's lips.

—*Percy Bysshe Shelly, poet*

When was the last time you heard someone say, "I love you!" without tagging on the inevitable (if unspoken) "as a friend." When was the last time you saw two people gazing into each other's eyes without thinking, Yeah right? When was the last time you heard someone announce, "I am truly, madly in love," without thinking, just wait until Monday morning . . . hardly the stuff we like to think about when we think about love but very much the stuff of the modern Manhattan relationship.

—CANDACE BUSHNELL, WRITER,
SEX AND THE CITY

I have found men who didn't know how to kiss.
I've always found time to teach them.

—*Mae West, actor*

People who throw kisses are hopelessly lazy.
—*Bob Hope, actor and entertainer*

To be in love is merely to be in a state
of perpetual anesthesia: To mistake an ordinary
young man for a Greek god or an ordinary
young woman for a goddess.
—*H. L. Mencken, journalist*

Many a man in love with a dimple makes
a mistake of marrying the whole girl.

—*Stephen Leacock, economist and humorist*

She walks in beauty,
Like the night of cloudless climes and starry skies;
And all that's best of dark and bright
Meet in her aspect and her eyes.

—*Lord Byron, poet*

Love teaches even asses to dance.

—*French proverb*

Love is only a dirty trick played on us
to achieve continuation of the species.

—*W. Somerset Maugham, writer*

Anyone can be passionate,
but it takes real lovers to be silly.

—*Rose Franken, writer*

Sex without love is as hollow
and ridiculous as love without sex.

—*Hunter S. Thompson, writer and journalist*

If love is blind, why is lingerie so popular?

—*Anonymous*

It does not matter what you do in
the bedroom as long as you do not do it
in the street and frighten the horses.

—*Mrs. Patrick Campbell, actor*

Marriage has many pains, but
celibacy has no pleasures.

—*Samuel Johnson, writer*

I need sex for a clear complexion,
but I'd rather do it for love.

—*Joan Crawford, actor*

Acting is not very hard. The most important
things are to be able to laugh and cry. If I have
to cry, I think of my sex life. And if I have to
laugh, well, I think of my sex life.

—*Glenda Jackson, politician and actor*

The big difference between
sex for money and sex for free is that sex
for money usually costs a lot less.

—*Brendan Behan, dramatist*

A lover without indiscretion is no lover at all.

—*Thomas Hardy, writer and poet*

The pleasure of love is in loving. We are happier in the passion we feel than in that we inspire.

—*François de la Rochefoucauld, writer and moralist*

❦

Happy are those lovers who, when their senses require rest, can fall back upon the intellectual enjoyments afforded by the mind! Sweet sleep then comes, and lasts until the body has recovered its general harmony. On awaking, the senses are again active and always ready to resume their action.

—*Giacomo Casanova, lover and writer*

❦

If we seek the pleasures of love, passion should be occasional, and common sense continual.

—*Robertson Davies, writer*

Love—a wildly misunderstood although
highly desirable malfunction of the heart
which weakens the brain, causes eyes to
sparkle, cheeks to glow, blood pressure
to rise and the lips to pucker.

—*Anonymous*

Love ain't nothing but sex misspelled.
—*Harlan Ellison, writer*

Women need a reason to have sex.
Men just need a place.
—*Billy Crystal, comedian and actor*

Sex alleviates tension. Love causes it.

—*Woody Allen, director and writer*

I have loved to the point of madness;
that which is called madness, that which to me,
is the only sensible way to love.

—*Françoise Sagan, writer and playwright*

My wife is a sex object—
every time I ask for sex, she objects.

—*Les Dawson, comedian*

Sex is a conversation carried out by other means. If you get on well out of bed, half the problems of bed are solved.

—*Peter Ustinov, actor*

I prefer love over sex.

—*Enrique Iglesias, singer*

I know nothing about sex, because I was always married.

—*Zsa Zsa Gabor, actor*

SIX:

Heartbreak

Is there any novel or movie worth its dramatic salt that doesn't include scenes of love that isn't returned or love that's faded and dying? When love is taken away or is unrequited, we can be devastated. The pain of heartbreak is all too real. But we're nothing if not resilient. After a time, most all of us will pick up the pieces and head out again, looking for love one more time.

You will never know true happiness until you
have truly loved, and you will never understand
what pain really is until you have lost it.

—*Anonymous*

Love never dies a natural death. It dies
because we don't know how to replenish its
source. It dies of blindness and errors and
betrayals. It dies of illness and wounds; it dies
of weariness, of withering, of tarnishing.

—*Anaïs Nin, writer*

Love built on beauty, soon as beauty, dies.

—John Donne, poet

Love lasts about seven years.
That's how long it takes for the cells of
the body to totally replace themselves.

—Françoise Sagan, writer and playwright

I hold it true, whate'er befall;

I feel it, when I sorrow most;

'Tis better to have loved and lost

Than never to have loved at all.

—alfred, Lord tennyson, poet

Ever has it been that love knows not
its own depth until the hour of separation.

—*Kahlil Gibran, poet*

⤬

I am a marvelous housekeeper.
Every time I leave a man I keep his house.

—*Zsa Zsa Gabor, actor*

⤬

Love is grand; divorce is a hundred grand.

—*Anonymous*

Love, the quest; marriage,
the conquest; divorce, the inquest.

—*Helen Rowland, humorist*

⌘

I was never one to patiently pick up broken
fragments and glue them together again and
tell myself that the mended whole was as good
as new. What is broken is broken—and
I'd rather remember it as it was at its best
than mend it and see the broken places
as long as I lived.

—*Margaret Mitchell, writer*

Nothing takes the
TASTE OUT OF PEANUT BUTTER

QUITE LIKE UNREQUITED LOVE.

—CHARLIE BROWN, peanuts

Happiness is the china shop; love is the bull.

—*H. L. Mencken, journalist*

An act of love that fails is just as much a part
of the divine life as an act of love that succeeds,
for love is measured by fullness, not by reception.

—*Harold Loukes, Christian educator and orator*

Love never dies of starvation,
but often of indigestion.

—*Ninon de Lenclos, French courtesan*

Have you ever been in love? Horrible isn't it?
It makes you so vulnerable. It opens your chest
and it opens up your heart and it means that
someone can get inside you and mess you up.

—*Neil Gaiman, writer*

You say that love is nonsense. . . . I tell you
it is no such thing. For weeks and months
it is a steady physical pain, an ache about
the heart, never leaving one, by night or by day;
a long strain on one's nerves like toothache or
rheumatism, not intolerable at any one instant,
but exhausting by its steady drain
on the strength.

—*Henry Brooks Adams, historian*

The greatest tragedy of life is not that
men perish, but that they cease to love.

—*W. Somerset Maugham, writer*

The way to love anything is
to realize that it might be lost.

—*G. K. Chesterton, writer*

Some of us think holding on makes us strong;
but sometimes it is letting go.

—*Hermann Hesse, writer*

Love is much like a wild rose, beautiful and calm, but willing to draw blood in its defense.

—*Mark Overby, writer*

Trouble is a part of life, and if you don't share it, you don't give the person who loves you enough chance to love you enough.

—*Dinah Shore, singer and actress*

It is not a lack of love, but a lack of friendship that makes unhappy marriages.

—*Friedrich Nietzsche, philosopher*

If you love someone, let them go. If they
return to you, it was meant to be. If they don't,
their love was never yours to begin with.

—*Anonymous*

Let no one who loves be called unhappy.
Even love unreturned has its rainbow.

—*J. M. Barrie, writer*

One reason people get divorced is
that they run out of gift ideas.

—*Robert Byrne, musician*

A mighty pain to love it is, and 'tis a pain
that pain to miss; but of all pains, the greatest
pain it is to love, but love in vain.

—*Abraham Cowley, poet*

How do you know love is gone?
If you said that you would be there at
seven and you get there by nine, and he
or she has not called the police—it's gone.

—*Marlene Dietrich, actor and singer*

Never seek to tell thy love,
Love that never told can be;
For the gentle wind doth move
Silently, invisibly.

I told my love, I told my love,
I told her all my heart,
Trembling, cold, in ghastly fears.
Ah! she did depart!

Soon after she was gone from me,
A traveller came by,
Silently, invisibly:
He took her with a sigh.
—*William Blake, poet*

I know that there are people who do not love
their fellow man, and I hate people like that!

—*Tom Lehrer, humorist*

When we lose one we love, our bitterest
tears are called forth by the memory of hours
when we loved not enough.

—*Maurice Maeterlinck, poet and essayist*

The Lord is close to those
whose hearts are breaking.

—*Psalms 34:18*

Heaven has no rage like love to hatred turned,
Nor hell a fury like a woman scorned.

—*William Congreve, playwright*

I'm very lonely now, Mary,
For the poor make no new friends;
But oh they love the better still
The few our Father sends!

—*Helen Selina, Lady Dufferin Sheridan, poet*

There is no sorrow like a love denied
Nor any joy like love that has its will.

—*Richard Hovey, writer*

If it hurts, it isn't love.

—*Chuck Spezzano, psychologist and writer*

He who has never experienced hurt,
cannot experience true love.

—*Tristan J. Loo, writer and mediator*

You know it's love when all you want
is that person to be happy, even if you're
not part of their happiness.

—*Julia Roberts, actor*

The heart that truly loves never forgets.

—Proverb

⚭

A divorce is like an amputation:
you survive it, but there's less of you.

—Margaret Atwood, writer

⚭

When two people decide to get a divorce, it isn't
a sign that they "don't understand" one another,
but a sign that they have, at last, begun to.

—Helen Rowland, humorist

⚭

The quarrels of lovers are the renewal of love.

—Terence, Roman playwright

Lips that taste of tears,
they say are the best for kissing.

—*Dorothy Parker, writer*

Though I know he loves me, tonight
my heart is sad; his kiss was not so
wonderful as all the dreams I had.

—*Sara Teasdale, poet*

When a love comes to an end, weaklings cry,
efficient ones instantly find another love,
and the wise already have one in reserve.

—*Oscar Wilde, playwright and writer*

There is a sacredness in tears.
They are not the mark of weakness, but
of power. They speak more eloquently than ten
thousand tongues. They are messengers of
overwhelming grief . . . and unspeakable love.

—*Washington Irving, writer*

❧

Love is a great poet, its resources are
inexhaustible, but if the end it has in view
is not obtained, it feels weary and remains silent.

—*Giacomo Casanova, lover and writer*

❧

Love is never lost. If not reciprocated,
it will flow back and soften and purify the heart.

—*Washington Irving, writer*

The heart is

THE ONLY BROKEN

INSTRUMENT THAT WORKS.

—t. e. kalem, critic

seven:

Introspection

IT'S BEEN SAID THAT WE CAN'T
LOVE ANOTHER UNTIL WE LEARN TO LOVE
OURSELVES. NOT THE NARCISSISTIC LOVE
THAT SEEKS A GLIMPSE OF ITSELF IN EVERY
MIRROR OR SHOP WINDOW WE PASS BUT
THE KIND OF LOVE THAT ENSURES THAT
WE TAKE CARE OF OURSELVES FIRST
BEFORE WE TAKE CARE OF OUR
FAMILY AND FRIENDS.

To love oneself is the
beginning of a life-long romance.
—*Oscar Wilde, playwright and writer*

∽

He that falls in love with
himself will have no rivals.
—*Benjamin Franklin, statesman*

∽

Love yourself first and
everything else falls into line.
—*Lucille Ball, actor*

Never pretend to a love which you do not actually feel, for love is not ours to command.

—*Alan Watts, philosopher*

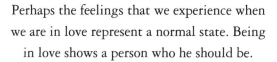

Perhaps the feelings that we experience when we are in love represent a normal state. Being in love shows a person who he should be.

—*Anton Chekhov, writer*

The love of liberty is the love of others; the love of power is the love of ourselves.

—*William Hazlitt, essayist*

Love is like playing the piano. First you must
learn to play by the rules, then you must forget
the rules and play from your heart.

—*Anonymous*

Love grows by giving. The love we give away
is the only love we keep. The only way
to retain love is to give it away.

—*Elbert Hubbard, writer and publisher*

Without love, benevolence becomes egotism.

—*Martin Luther King, Jr., civil rights leader*

You cannot be lonely if you like
the person you're alone with.
—*Wayne W. Dyer, motivational
speaker and writer*

Relish love in your old age!
Aged love is like aged wine;
it becomes more satisfying,
more refreshing, more
valuable, more appreciated
and more intoxicating!
—*Leo Buscaglia, writer
and speaker*

Guard within yourself that treasure, kindness.
Know how to give without hesitation,
how to lose without regret, how to acquire
without meanness; know how to replace
in your heart, by the happiness of those you love,
the happiness that may be wanting to yourself.

—*George Sand, writer*

If it is a virtue to love my neighbor as a human
being, it must be a virtue—and not a vice—to
love myself, since I am a human being too.

—*Erich Fromm, psychoanalyst and writer*

Since love grows within you, so beauty grows.
For love is the beauty of the soul.

—*St. Augustine, theologian*

Self-love, my liege, is not so vile
a sin as self-neglecting.

—*William Shakespeare, playwright and poet*

Out of love you can speak with straight fury.

—*Eudora Welty, writer*

Whate'er th' Almighty's subsequent command,
His first command is this—"Man, love thyself."
—Edward Young, poet

❦

Self-love seems so often unrequited.
—Anthony Powell, writer

❦

Love is, above all else, the gift of oneself.
—Jean Anouilh, dramatist

You yourself,

AS MUCH AS ANYBODY IN

THE ENTIRE UNIVERSE,

DESERVE YOUR LOVE AND

AFFECTION.

—BUDDHA (SIDDHARTHA GAUTAMA),
RELIGIOUS FIGURE

A heart that loves is always young.

—*Greek proverb*

∽

Who so loves, believes the impossible.

—*Elizabeth Barrett Browning, poet*

∽

Accept the things
To which fate binds you and
Love the people with whom fate
Brings you together
But do so with all your heart.

—*Marcus Aurelius, emperor*

Have you ever been at sea in a dense fog,
when it seemed as if a tangible white darkness
shut you in and the great ship, tense and
anxious, groped her way toward the shore with
plummet and sounding-line, and you waited
with beating heart for something to happen?
I was like that ship before my education began,
only I was without compass or sounding line,
and no way of knowing how near the harbor was.
"Light! Give me light!" was the wordless
cry of my soul, and the light of love shone
on me in that very hour.

—*Helen Keller, activist*

Love can be understood only
"from the inside," as a language
can be understood only by someone
who speaks it, as a world can be
understood only by someone
who lives in it.

—*Robert C. Solomon, philosopher*

eight:

Possessions

Besides loving our fellow man and woman, many of us profess love for our pets, our cats and dogs and other living, breathing animals. It is also possible to love *things*, inanimate objects that are in no position to return our love even if they wanted to. It could be something to eat: a prime rib dinner, a chocolate soda, or the first fresh corn of the season. It might be that favorite vacation spot: Hawaii, the south of France, or Disneyworld. And when we love our country, many are prepared to pay a tremendous price, the ultimate price, in its name.

Dogs have more love than integrity.
They've been true to us, yes, but they
haven't been true to themselves.

—*Clarence Day, writer*

Love me, love my dog.

—*John Heywood, dramatist*

It's just the most amazing thing to love a dog,
isn't it? It makes our relationships with people
seem as boring as a bowl of oatmeal.

—*John Grogan, columnist and writer*

The better I get to know men,
the more I find myself loving dogs.
—*Charles de Gaulle, political leader*

Love for a dog during childhood is one
of the deepest and purest emotions we are
ever likely to have, and it remains with us
for the rest of our lives. For some people,
their first experience with love is with a dog.
The fact that the dog returns the love
so fiercely, so openly, so unambivalently,
is for many children a unique
and lasting experience.
—*Jeffrey Moussaieff Masson, writer*

Dogs love their friends and bite their enemies, quite unlike people, who are incapable of pure love and always have to mix love and hate in their . . . relations.

—*Sigmund Freud, psychiatrist*

❧

I really love pets. They're like children. They know if you really love them or not. You can't fool them.

—*Donna Douglas, actor*

❧

There is no reciprocity. Men love women, women love children, children love hamsters.

—*Alice Thomas Ellis (aka Anna Haycraft), writer*

Love conquers all things
except poverty and a toothache.

—*Mae West, actor*

Be unselfish in your love.
Remember, you are not the cat.

—*Bill Zimmerman, journalist and editor*

There is no love sincerer
than the love of food.

—*George Bernard Shaw,
writer and critic*

When a man is small, he loves and hates food with a ferocity which soon dims. At six years old his very bowels will heave when such a dish as creamed carrots or cold tapioca appear before him.

—M.F.K. Fisher, *writer and gourmand*

$\mathcal{I}$f you sweep a house, and tend its
fires and fill its stove, and there
is love in you all the years you are
doing this, then you and that house
are married, that house is yours.

—TRUMAN CAPOTE, WRITER

Anything will give up its secrets
if you love it enough.

—*George Washington Carver, inventor and botanist*

I love Mickey Mouse more than any woman
I've ever known.

—*Walt Disney, animator and entrepreneur*

I'm not a vegetarian because I love animals.
I'm a vegetarian because I hate plants.

—*A. Whitney Brown, comedian*

Man has bought brains, but all the millions in the world have failed to buy love. Man has subdued bodies, but all the power on earth has been unable to subdue love. Man has conquered whole nations, but all his armies could not conquer love. Man has chained and fettered the spirit, but he has been utterly helpless before love. Thus love has the magic power to make of a beggar a king.

—Emma Goldman, political activist

Love lasteth long as the money endureth.

—William Caxton, printer

It is good to love the unknown.

—Charles Lamb, critic and essayist

If it's true that men are such beasts,
this must account for the fact
that most women are animal lovers.
—*Doris Day, actor and animal advocate*

If we love our country,
we should also love our countrymen.
—*Ronald Reagan, U.S. president and actor*

NINE:

Faith

As wonderful as love is among men, women, friends, and family, unfortunately, it is not always unconditional. Even with the best of intentions we withhold love, or love is withheld from us. But for those of us with faith, divine love— love from God—is always there for us, no matter what we think, say, or do.

Love means to commit oneself without guarantee, to give oneself completely in the hope that our love will produce love in the loved person. Love is an act of faith, and whoever is of little faith is also of little love.

—*Erich Fromm, psychoanalyst and writer*

Above all things have devoted love among yourselves, for love covers a multitude of sins.

—*1 Peter 4:8*

Love one another and you will be happy.
It's as simple and as difficult as that.

—*Michael Leunig, cartoonist*

Because God is love, the most important lesson
He wants you to learn on earth is how to love.

—*Rick Warren, pastor and writer*

Love is not blind—it sees more, not less.
But because it sees more, it is willing to see less.

—*Julius Gordon, writer*

Since love grows within you,
so beauty grows. For love is
the beauty of the soul.

—*St. Augustine, theologian*

If you judge people,
you have no time to love them.

—*Mother Teresa, humanitarian*

$\mathcal{I}$t is a curious subject of
observation and inquiry, whether
hatred and love be not the same thing
at bottom. Each, in its utmost
development, supposes a high degree
of intimacy and heart-knowledge;
each renders one individual dependent
for the food of his affections and
spiritual life upon another: each leaves
the passionate lover, or the no less
passionate hater, forlorn and desolate
by the withdrawal of his subject.
Philosophically considered, therefore,
the two passions seem essentially
the same, except that one happens
to be seen in a celestial radiance,
and the other in a dusky
and lurid glow.

—NATHANIEL HAWTHORNE, WRITER

All, everything that I understand, I understand only because I love. Everything is, everything exists, only because I love. Everything is united by it alone. Love is God, and to die means that I, a particle of love, shall return to the general and eternal source.

—Prince Andrew in *Leo Tolstoy's* War and Peace

Paradise is always where love dwells.

—*Jean Paul F. Richter, actor*

When we feel love and kindness toward others, it not only makes others feel loved and cared for, but it helps us also to develop inner happiness and peace.

—the Dalai Lama, Religious Leader

Your body needs to be held and to hold, to be touched and to touch. None of these needs is to be despised, denied, or repressed. But you have to keep searching for your body's deeper need, the need for genuine love. Every time you are able to go beyond the body's superficial desires for love, you are bringing your body home and moving toward integration and unity.

—*Henri Nouwen, priest and writer*

Jesus said unto him, Thou shalt love the Lord thy God with all thy heart, and with all thy soul, and with all thy mind. This is the first and great commandment. And the second is like unto it, Thou shalt love thy neighbour as thyself. On these two commandments hang all the law and the prophets.

—*Matthew 22:34–40*

The mystery of love is greater
than the mystery of death.

—*Anonymous*

Hatred paralyzes life; love releases it.
Hatred confuses life; love harmonizes it.
Hatred darkens life; love illumines it.
—*Martin Luther King, Jr., civil rights leader*

Whenever you are confronted
with an opponent, conquer him with love.
—*Mahatma Gandhi, political leader and activist*

Time is too slow for those who wait, too swift
for those who fear, too long for those who grieve,
too short for those who rejoice, but for those
who love, time is eternity.

—*Henry Van Dyke, clergyman and writer*

Nobody has ever measured, not even poets,
how much the heart can hold.

—*Zelda Fitzgerald, writer*

Tell me who admires and loves you,
and I will tell you who you are.

—*Charles-Augustin Sainte-Beuve, historian*

I have been astonished that men
could die martyrs for their religion—
I have shudder'd at it.
I shudder no more.
I could be martyr'd for my religion
Love is my religion
And I could die for that.
I could die for you.

—*John Keats, poet*

Bitterness imprisons life; love releases it.
Bitterness paralyzes life; love empowers it.
Bitterness sours life; love sweetens it.
Bitterness sickens life; love heals it.
Bitterness blinds life; love anoints its eyes.

—*Harry Emerson Fosdick, clergyman*

No cord nor cable can so forcibly draw, or hold
so fast, as love can do with a twined thread.

—Robert Burton, scholar and theologian

∽

I believe that life is given us so that we may
grow in love, and I believe that God is in me as
the sun is in the color and fragrance of a flower.

—Helen Keller, activist

There is only one path to Heaven.
On Earth, we call it Love.

—*Karen Goldman, writer*

Treasure the love you receive above all.
It will survive long after your gold
and good health have vanished.

—*Og Mandino, writer and lecturer*

$\mathcal{L}$ove is the vital essence that

pervades and permeates,

from the centre to the

circumference, the graduating

circles of all thought and action.

Love is the talisman of

human weal and woe—the open

sesame to every soul.

—ELIZABETH CADY STANTON,
SOCIAL REFORMER

Give all to love; obey thy heart.

—*Ralph Waldo Emerson, philosopher*

'Tis the most tender part of love,
each other to forgive.

—*John Sheffield, poet*

Never forget the three powerful resources
you always have available to you: love,
prayer and forgiveness.

—*H. Jackson Brown, Jr., writer*

Love blinds us to faults, hatred to virtues.

—*Moses Ibn Ezra, philosopher and poet*

Agape is disinterested love. . . . Agape does
not begin by discriminating between worthy
and unworthy people, or any qualities people
possess. It begins by loving others for their
sakes. . . . Therefore, agape makes
no distinction between friend and enemy;
it is directed toward both.

—*Martin Luther King, Jr., civil rights leader*

Do not waste time bothering whether you "love" your neighbor; act as if you did. As soon as we do this we find one of the great secrets. When you are behaving as if you loved someone, you will presently come to love him. If you injure someone you dislike, you will find yourself disliking him more. If you do him a good turn, you will find yourself disliking him less.

—*C. S. Lewis, writer*

We are obliged to love one another. We are not strictly bound to "like" one another.

—*Thomas Merton, writer and poet*

To love one's neighbors, to love one's enemies,
to love everything—to love God in all His
manifestations—human love serves to love
those dear to us but to love one's enemies
we need divine love.

—*Leo Tolstoy, writer and philosopher*

❦

Love is what we were borne with.
Fear is what we learned here.

—*Marianne Williamson, writer and peace activist*

❦

Understanding is the essence of love.

—*Thich Nhat Hanh, Buddhist monk and writer*

The higher animals are in a sense drawn
into Man when he loves them and makes them
(as he does) much more nearly human
than they would otherwise be.

—*C. S. Lewis, writer*

He that loveth his brother abideth in the light,
and there is none occasion of stumbling in him.

—*1 John 2:10*

Beloved, let us love one another: for love
is of God; and every one that loveth
is born of God, and knoweth God.

—*1 John 4:7*

We're born alone, we live alone,
we die alone. Only through our love and
friendship can we create the illusion for the
moment that we're not alone.

—*Orson Welles, actor and filmmaker*

Love and work are the
cornerstones of our humanness.

—*Sigmund Freud, psychiatrist*

That best portion of a good man's life,
His little, nameless, unremembered acts
Of kindness and of love.

—*William Wordsworth, poet*

A thing of beauty is a joy forever;
Its loveliness increases; it will never
Pass into nothingness.

—John Keats, poet

God loves us the way we are,
but too much to leave us that way.

—Leighton Ford, evangelist

Though our feelings come and go,
God's love for us does not.

—C. S. Lewis, writer

Love is a fruit in season at all times,
and within reach of every hand.

—*Mother Teresa, humanitarian*

All wise people say the same thing;
that you are deserving of love, and that it's
all here now, everything you need. When you
pray, you are not starting the conversation
from scratch, just remembering to plug back
into a conversation that's always in progress.

—*Anne Lamott, writer*

Speak to me of love, said St Francis
to the almond tree, and the tree blossomed.

—*Nicholas Kazantzakis, writer*

ten:

Life

THE GREATEST GIFT EACH OF US RECEIVES
WHEN WE ARE BORN IS THE GIFT OF LIFE.
REGARDLESS OF HOW MANY DAYS WE'RE
GRANTED, LIFE IS SO MUCH SWEETER
WITH THE GIFT OF LOVE, WHETHER WE ARE
THE GIVER OR THE RECEIVER. AT THE HEART
OF THIS IS THE LOVE OF LIFE ITSELF, THE JOIE
DE VIVRE THAT'S OFTEN SO HARD TO MAINTAIN
IN THE FACE OF LIFE'S DAILY GRIND.
WHEN WE CAN STOP TO LOOK AROUND
AND SEEK IT OUT, LOVE REALLY
IS EVERYWHERE.

In our life there is a single color, as on an artist's palette, which provides the meaning of life and art. It is the color of love.

—*Marc Chagall, artist*

In our life there is a single color, as on an artist's palette, which provides the meaning of life and art. It is the color of love.

Dost thou love life? Then do not squander time, for that is the stuff life is made of.

—*Benjamin Franklin, statesman*

Keep love in your heart. A life without it is like a sunless garden when the flowers are dead.

—*Oscar Wilde, playwright and writer*

To fear love is to fear life, and those
who fear life are already three parts dead.
—*Bertrand Russell, philosopher and mathematician*

We are most alive when we're in love.
—*John Updike, writer and critic*

For one human being to love another:
that is perhaps the most difficult of our tasks;
the ultimate, the last test and proof,
the work for which all other work is but
preparation.
—*Rainer Maria Rilke, poet*

And whatever it is that keeps widening
your heart, that's Mary, too, not only the
power inside you but the love. And when you
get down to it, Lily, that's the only purpose
grand enough for a human life. Not just
to love—but to *persist* in love.
—*Sue Monk Kidd, writer,* The Secret Life of Bees

Where there is love there is life.
—*Mahatma Gandhi, political leader and activist*

Loving people live in a loving world. Hostile
people live in a hostile world. Same world.
—*Wayne W. Dyer, motivational speaker and writer*

Neither a lofty degree of intelligence
nor imagination nor both together go to
the making of genius. Love, love, love,
that is the soul of genius.

—*Wolfgang Amadeus Mozart, composer*

Love is like pi—natural,
irrational, and very important.

—*Lisa Hoffman, writer*

We've got this gift of love,

but love is like a precious plant.

You can't just accept it and leave

it in the cupboard or just think it's

going to get on by itself. You've got

to keep watering it. You've got

to really look after it and

nurture it.

—JOHN LENNON,
MUSICIAN AND SONGWRITER

What the world really needs is
more love and less paperwork.
—*Pearl Bailey, actor and singer*

I love humanity but I hate people.
—*Edna St. Vincent Millay, poet*

To live is like to love—all reason is
against it, and all healthy instinct for it.
—*Samuel Butler, writer*

Life without love is like a tree
without blossom and fruit.
—*Kahlil Gibran, poet*

Love looks through a telescope;
envy through a microscope.
—*Josh Billings, essayist and humorist*

In the arithmetic of love, one plus one equals
everything, and two minus one equals nothing.
—*Mignon McLaughlin, journalist*

There is only one happiness in life:
to love and be loved.

—*George Sand, writer*

To love means not to impose your own powers
on your fellow man but offer him your help.
And if he refuses it, to be proud
that he can do it on his own strength.

—*Elisabeth Kübler-Ross, physician and writer*

Love is like the truth, sometimes it prevails,
sometimes it hurts.

—*Victor M. Garcia, Jr., writer*

If love is the answer, could you please
rephrase the question?

—*Lily Tomlin, actor and comedian*

The Grand essentials of happiness are:
something to do, something to love,
and something to hope for.

—*Allan K. Chalmers, writer*

The love of life is necessary to the vigorous
prosecution of any undertaking.

—*Samuel Johnson, writer*

Love is the master key which opens
the gates of happiness.

—*Oliver Wendell Holmes, Sr., physician and writer*

I have been so great a lover: filled my days
So proudly with the splendour of Love's praise,
The pain, the calm, and the astonishment,
Desire illimitable, and silent content,
And all dear names men use, to cheat despair,
For the perplexed and viewless streams that bear
Our hearts at random down the dark of life.

—*Rupert Brooke, poet, "The Great Lover"*

The one thing we can never get
enough of is love. And the one thing
we never give enough of is love.

—*Henry Miller, writer*

∽

There can be no peace of mind in love,
since the advantage one has secured is never
anything by a fresh starting-point
for further desires.

—*Marcel Proust, writer*

∽

What I cannot love, I overlook.

—*Anaïs Nin, writer*

A loving relationship is one in which
the loved one is free to be himself—to laugh
with me, but never at me; to cry with me, but
never because of me; to love life, to love himself,
to love being loved. Such a relationship
is based upon freedom and can never grow
in a jealous heart.

—*Leo Buscaglia, writer and speaker*

Love is a canvas furnished by nature
and embroidered by imagination.

—*Voltaire, writer*

"Have I told you about the tension of opposites?" he says. The tension of opposites? "Life is a series of pulls back and forth. You want to do one thing, but you are bound to do something else. Something hurts you, yet you know it shouldn't. You take certain things for granted, even when you know you should never take anything for granted. A tension of opposites, like a pull on a rubber band. And most of us live somewhere in the middle." Sounds like a wrestling match, I say. "A wrestling match." He laughs. "Yes, you could describe life that way." So which side wins, I ask? "Which side wins?" He smiles at me, the crinkled eyes, the crooked teeth. "Love wins. Love always wins."

—MORRIE SCHWARTZ IN MITCH ALBOM'S
TUESDAYS WITH MORRIE

Love is the only sane and satisfactory
answer to the problem of human existence.

—*Erich Fromm, psychoanalyst and writer*

∽∾

We are all born for love; it is the
principle of existence and its only end.

—*Benjamin Disraeli, British, political leader*

∽∾

Love is the only thing that we can carry with
us when we go, and it makes the end so easy.

—*Louisa May Alcott, writer and reformer*

Among those whom I like or admire, I can find
no common denominator, but among those
whom I love, I can: all of them make me laugh.

—*W. H. Auden, poet and writer*

Life isn't long enough for love and art.

—*W. Somerset Maugham, writer*

The essence of love is kindness.

—*Robert Louis Stevenson, writer*

Love . . . includes fellowship in
suffering, in joy and in effort.
—*Albert Schweitzer, physician and philosopher*

When the power of love overcomes the
love of power, the world will know peace.
—*Jimi Hendrix, musician*

Love is anterior to life
Posterior to death
Initial of creation, and
The exponent of breath.
—*Emily Dickinson, poet*

Who will tell whether one happy
moment of love or the joy of breathing
or walking on a bright morning and smelling
the fresh air, is not worth all the suffering
and effort which life implies.

—*Erich Fromm, psychoanalyst and writer*

Be glad of life because it gives you the
chance to love and to work and to play
and to look up at the stars.

—*Henry Van Dyke, clergyman and writer*

Love is ever the beginning of
Knowledge as fire is of light.

—*Thomas Carlyle, historian*

Life in common among people who love
each other is the ideal of happiness.

—*George Sand, writer*

∽⧬∾

I wonder what memories of yours will persist
as you go on in life. My hunch is that the most
important will have to do with feelings
of loving and being loved—whoever's been
close to you. As you continue to grow,
you'll find many ways of expressing your love
and you'll discover more and more ways
in which others express their love for you.

—*Fred Rogers, Mister Rogers' Neighborhood*

∽⧬∾

Where love is, no room is too small.

—*Talmud*

If music be the food of love, play on;
Give me excess of it, that, surfeiting,
The appetite may sicken, and so die.
That strain again! it had a dying fall:
O, it came o'er my ear like the sweet sound.

—*William Shakespeare, playwright and poet*

They say a person needs just three things
to be truly happy in this world: someone to love,
something to do, and something to hope for.

—*Tom Bodett, writer and radio host*

To live in this world, you

must be able to do three things:

to love what is mortal; to hold it

against your bones knowing your

own life depends on it; and, when the

time comes to let it go, to let it go.

—MARY OLIVER, POET

It is love, not reason, that is stronger than death.

—*Thomas Mann, writer*

⚬

Love feels no burden, regards not labors,
strives toward more than it attains, argues not
of impossibility, since it believes that it may
and can do all things. Therefore it avails
for all things, and fulfils and accomplishes
much where one not a lover falls
and lies helpless.

—*Thomas à Kempis, monk and mystic*

⚬

Love your neighbor as yourself,
but don't take down the fence.

—*Carl Sandburg, poet*

There is no better exercise for strengthening the
heart than reaching down and lifting up another.

—*Anonymous*

Love does not dominate; it cultivates.

—*Johann Wolfgang von Goethe, poet*

Life is pain and the enjoyment of love
is an anesthetic.

—*Cesare Pavese, writer and poet*

Love is letting go of fear.

—*Gerald Jampolsky, psychiatrist and writer*

If we all discovered that we only
had five minutes left to say all that we
wanted to say, every telephone booth
would be occupied by people
calling other people to tell them
that they loved them.

—*Christopher Morley, writer and editor*

Love doesn't make the world go round,
Love is what makes the ride worthwhile.

—*Elizabeth Barrett Browning, poet*

Age does not protect you from love. But love,
to some extent, protects you from age.

—*Jeanne Moreau, actor and writer*

And remember, my sentimental friend,
that a heart is not judged by how
much you love, but by how much you
are loved by others.

—*L. Frank Baum, writer,* The Wizard of Oz

Love's like the measles—all the worse
when it comes late in life.

—*Douglas Jerrold, humorist and playwright*

eLeveN:

True Love

You can't measure love, nor can you adequately describe it to another person. Perhaps more than any other emotion, you know it when you feel it. You'll know when you've found your soul mate, when you really do want to spend the rest of your life with someone, when you look at your child and you just can't breathe for loving him or her, when your mind and your being are at one with what you believe. This is true love, the greatest love of all.

True love is like ghosts, which everybody
talks about and few have seen.
—*François de la Rochefoucauld, writer and moralist*

∽

True love is eternal, infinite, and always
like itself. It is equal and pure, without violent
demonstrations: it is seen with white hairs
and is always young in the heart.
—*Honoré de Balzac, writer*

Generally, by the time you are Real,
most of your hair has been loved off, and
your eyes drop out and you get loose
in the joints and very shabby. But these
things don't matter at all, because once you
are Real you can't be ugly, except to
people who don't understand.

—*Margery Williams,*
writer, The Velveteen Rabbit

All kings, and all their favourites,

All glory of honours, beauties, wits,

The sun itself, which makes time, as they pass,

Is elder by a year now than it was

When thou and I first one another saw.

All other things to their destruction draw,

Only our love hath no decay;

This no to-morrow hath, nor yesterday;

Running it never runs from us away,

But truly keeps his first, last, everlasting day.

—*John Donne, poet*

$\mathcal{T}$ime is too slow for those who

wait, too swift for those who fear,

too long for those who grieve,

too short for those who rejoice, but

for those who love, time is eternity.

—HENRY VAN DYKE,
CLERGYMAN AND WRITER

Love looks not with the eyes, but with the mind;
And therefore is winged Cupid painted blind.

—*William Shakespeare, playwright and poet*

∽

True love brings up everything—you're allowing
a mirror to be held up to you daily.

—*Jennifer Aniston, actor*

∽

Perfect love is rare indeed—for to be a lover
will require that you continually have the
subtlety of the very wise, the flexibility
of the child, the sensitivity of the artist,
the understanding of the philosopher, the
acceptance of the saint, the tolerance of the
scholar and the fortitude of the certain.

—*Leo Buscaglia, writer and speaker*

The course of true love never did run smooth.

—*William Shakespeare, playwright and poet*

⌘

True love is night jasmine, a diamond
in darkness, the heartbeat no cardiologist
has ever heard. It is the most common
of miracles, fashioned of fleecy clouds—
a handful of stars tossed into the night sky.

—*Jim Bishop, columnist and historian*

⌘

Some love lasts a lifetime. True love lasts forever.

—*Anonymous*

What the heart gives away is never gone.
. . . It is kept in the hearts of others.
—*Robin St. John, writer*

Being deeply loved by someone
gives you strength, while loving someone
deeply gives you courage.
—*Lao Tzu, philosopher*

Love me without fear
Trust me without questioning
Need me without demanding
Want me without restrictions
Accept me without change
Desire me without inhibitions
For a love so free . . .
Will never fly away.
—*Dick Sutphen, writer*

The Eskimo has fifty-two names for
snow because it is important to them;
there ought to be as many for love.
—*Margaret Atwood, writer*

A romp in the hay lingers like the first
line of a song, but your true love is the one
you make a life with and write more than a
line about, you write a whole book.

—*Garrison Keillor, Writer,* Love Me

The greatest happiness in life is the conviction
that we are loved—loved for ourselves, or rather,
loved in spite of ourselves.

—*Victor Hugo, writer*

I love thee, I love but thee
With a love that shall not die
Till the sun grows cold
And the stars grow old.

—*William Shakespeare, playwright and poet*

WESTLEY: "I told you I would always come for you. Why didn't you wait for me?"

BUTTERCUP: "Well . . . you were dead."

WESTLEY: "Death cannot stop true love. All it can do is delay it for a while."

—*William Goldman, screenwriter,*
The Princess Bride

True love is the only heart disease that is best left to "run on"—the only affection of the heart for which there is no help, and none desired.

—*Mark Twain, writer and humorist*

True love's the gift which God has given
To man alone beneath the heaven:
It is not fantasy's hot fire,
Whose wishes soon as granted fly;
It liveth not in fierce desire.

—*Sir Walter Scott, writer and poet*

To love and be loved is to
feel the sun from both sides.

—*David Viscott, writer*

Do you want me to tell you something really subversive? Love is everything it's cracked up to be. That's why people are so cynical about it. . . . It really is worth fighting for, being brave for, risking everything for. And the trouble is, if you don't risk everything, you risk even more.

—*Erica Jong, writer and poet*

The best and most beautiful
things in the world cannot be seen or
even touched—they must be felt
with the heart.

—HELEN KELLER, ACTIVIST

I love thee to the depth and breadth and height
my soul can reach.

—*Elizabeth Barrett Browning, poet*

⧬

The truth [is] that there is only one terminal
dignity—love. And the story of a love
is not important—what is important
is that one is capable of love. It is perhaps
the only glimpse we are permitted of eternity.

—*Helen Hayes, actor*

⧬

Love is always bestowed as a gift—freely,
willingly and without expectation.
We don't love to be loved; we love to love.

—*Leo Buscaglia, writer and speaker*

The chemist who can extract from
his heart's elements compassion, respect,
longing, patience, regret, surprise, and
forgiveness and compound them into one
can create that atom which is called love.

—*Kahlil Gibran, poet*

True love cannot be found
where it truly does not exist,
nor can it be hidden where it truly does.

—*Anonymous*

Love conquers all.

—*Virgil, poet*

True love begins when
nothing is looked for in return.

—*Antoine de Saint-Exupéry,*

writer

Speaker List

one: family

Agatha Christie
Frank Pittman
Stephanie Marston
Henry Ward Beecher
Winston Churchill
William Saroyan
Ernest Havemann
Eva Burrows
Friedrich Nietzsche
Marge Kennedy/Janet
  Spencer King
Gabriel García Márquez
Giuseppe Mazzini
Mother Teresa
William Butler Yeats
Robert Orben
George Burns

Stephanie Marston
Lewis Mumford
Lois Wyse
Daphne
Oscar Wilde
Abraham Lincoln
Welsh proverb
Sam Levenson
Henry Ward Beecher

two: friends

Frances Farmer
Elbert Hubbard
George Herbert
Barbara Kingsolver
Judith Crist
Samuel Richardson
Chinese proverb

John 15:13
A. A. Milne
Richard Bach
Jane Austen
Samuel Taylor Coleridge
Hilaire Belloc
Elie Wiesel
Ella Wheeler Wilcox
Ambrose Bierce
Thyra Samter Winslow
Mason Cooley
Anonymous
Lord Byron
Mary Wollstonecraft
Anna Quindlen
Anita Brookner
Oscar Wilde
François de la
   Rochefoucauld
Molière
Robert Louis Stevenson
Charles Caleb Colton
Christian H. Godefroy

Babe Didrikson Zaharias
Euripides
Sydney Smith

tHRee:
BeGINNINGS

Mary Wilson Little
Sam Levenson
W. Somerset Maugham
Anne-Sophie Swetchine
Albert Einstein
D. H. Lawrence
Honoré de Balzac
Plato
Dorothy Parker
Mark Twain
Anonymous
Helen Rowland
Alice Walker
Renee Zellweger
Charles Baudelaire
Fitzwilliam Darcy

Bertrand Russell

Albert Ellis

Clark Gable

Henny Youngman

Thomas Campbell

Ellye Howell Glover

Marie von Ebner-
  Eschenbach

Emily Brontë

Woody Allen

Jule Renard

Albert Einstein

Ursula K. Le Guin

Isak Dinesen

Romeo

four:

companionship

Alan King

Miss Piggy

André Maurois

W. Somerset Maugham

Paul Tillich

Anonymous

Lester Pearson

Peter Ustinov

Winston Churchill

Joanne Woodward

Amy Bloom

Antoine de Saint-Exupéry

Aristotle

Barbara Bush

Philip Barry

Rollo May

David Bissonette

Melanie Clark

Elizabeth Bowen

Anonymous

Mark Twain

Keith Sullivan

Groucho Marx

Mae West

Rita Rudner

W. Somerset Maugham

Agatha Christie

Alexandre Dumas

Helen Rowland

Benjamin Franklin

Joan Davis

Erma Bombeck

Marnie Reed Crowell

Estée Lauder

Mark Twain

Marge Kennedy

Erich Segal

Judith Viorst

Benjamin Franklin
  (Hawkeye) Pierce

Ben Hecht

Bruce Lee

Tom Robbins

V. F. Calverton

Harry Burns

Muriel Spark

Jonathan Swift

Rita Rudner

William Cowper

Josh Billings

Ellen Key

Muhammad

Talmud

Fannie Flagg

Benton Fraser

Talmud

Francis Beaumont/John
  Fletcher

Robert Burns

Charles Jefferys

Caroline Rhea

Shelley Winters

Woody Allen

Lyndon B. Johnson

Groucho Marx

Gloria Steinem

Henny Youngman

Gloria Swanson

Morton Hunt

Norman Mailer

Anonymous

Irish proverb

Edgar Watson Howe

Mort Sahl

Marjorie Kinnan Rawlings

William Parrish

Nancy Reagan

Hugh Walpole

five: passion

Lao Tzu

Ally McBeal

Nora Ephron

Billy Connolly

Don Byas

Joss Whedon

Friedrich Nietzsche

Ice T

Lynda Barry

Thomas Carlyle

Robert Frost

Ingrid Bergman

Percy Bysshe Shelly

Candace Bushnell

Mae West

Bob Hope

H. L. Mencken

Stephen Leacock

Lord Byron

French proverb

W. Somerset Maugham

Rose Franken

Hunter S. Thompson

Anonymous

Mrs. Patrick Campbell

Samuel Johnson

Joan Crawford

Glenda Jackson

Brendan Behan

Thomas Hardy

François de la
    Rochefoucauld

Giacomo Casanova

Robertson Davies

Anonymous

Harlan Ellison

Billy Crystal

Woody Allen

Françoise Sagan
Les Dawson
Peter Ustinov
Enrique Iglesias
Zsa Zsa Gabor

SIX: Heartbreak

Anonymous
Anaïs Nin
John Donne
Françoise Sagan
Alfred, Lord Tennyson
Kahlil Gibran
Zsa Zsa Gabor
Anonymous
Helen Rowland
Margaret Mitchell
Charlie Brown
H. L. Mencken
Harold Loukes
Ninon de Lenclos

Neil Gaiman
Henry Brooks Adams
W. Somerset Maugham
G. K. Chesterton
Hermann Hesse
Mark Overby
Dinah Shore
Friedrich Nietzsche
Anonymous
J. M. Barrie
Robert Byrne
Abraham Cowley
Marlene Dietrich
William Blake
Tom Lehrer
Maurice Maeterlinck
Psalms 34:18
William Congreve
Helen Selina, Lady
   Dufferin Sheridan
Richard Hovey
Chuck Spezzano

Tristan J. Loo
Julia Roberts
Proverb
Margaret Atwood
Helen Rowland
Terence
Dorothy Parker
Sara Teasdale
Oscar Wilde
Washington Irving
Giacomo Casanova
Washington Irving
T. E. Kalem

seven:
introspection

Oscar Wilde
Benjamin Franklin
Lucille Ball
Alan Watts
Anton Chekhov

William Hazlitt
Anonymous
Elbert Hubbard
Martin Luther King, Jr.
Wayne W. Dyer
Leo Buscaglia
George Sand
Erich Fromm
St. Augustine
William Shakespeare
Eudora Welty
Edward Young
Anthony Powell
Jean Anouilh
Buddha (Siddhartha
    Gautama)
Greek proverb
Elizabeth Barrett
    Browning
Marcus Aurelius
Helen Keller
Robert C. Solomon

eight:

possessions

Clarence Day
John Heywood
John Grogan
Charles de Gaulle
Jeffrey Moussaieff Masson
Sigmund Freud
Donna Douglas
Alice Thomas Ellis
  (aka Anna Haycraft)
Mae West
Bill Zimmerman
George Bernard Shaw
M.F.K. Fisher
Truman Capote
George Washington
  Carver
Walt Disney
A. Whitney Brown
Emma Goldman
William Caxton

Charles Lamb
Doris Day
Ronald Reagan

nine: faith

Erich Fromm
1 Peter 4:8
Michael Leunig
Rick Warren
Julius Gordon
St. Augustine
Mother Teresa
Nathaniel Hawthorne
Prince Andrew
Jean Paul F. Richter
The Dalai Lama
Henri Nouwen
Matthew 22:34–40
Anonymous
Martin Luther King, Jr.
Mahatma Gandhi
Henry Van Dyke

Zelda Fitzgerald
Charles-Augustin
  Sainte-Beuve
John Keats
Harry Emerson Fosdick
Robert Burton
Helen Keller
Karen Goldman
Og Mandino
Elizabeth Cady Stanton
Ralph Waldo Emerson
John Sheffield
H. Jackson Brown, Jr.
Moses Ibn Ezra
Martin Luther King, Jr.
C. S. Lewis
Thomas Merton
Leo Tolstoy
Marianne Williamson
Thich Nhat Hanh
C. S. Lewis
1 John 2:10
1 John 4:7

Orson Welles
Sigmund Freud
William Wordsworth
John Keats
Leighton Ford
C. S. Lewis
Mother Teresa
Anne Lamott
Nicholas Kazantzakis

ten: Life

Marc Chagall
Benjamin Franklin
Oscar Wilde
Bertrand Russell
John Updike
Rainer Maria Rilke
Sue Monk Kidd
Mahatma Gandhi
Wayne W. Dyer
Wolfgang Amadeus
  Mozart

Lisa Hoffman
John Lennon
Pearl Bailey
Edna St. Vincent Millay
Samuel Butler
Kahlil Gibran
Josh Billings
Mignon McLaughlin
George Sand
Elisabeth Kübler-Ross
Victor M. Garcia, Jr.
Lily Tomlin
Allan K. Chalmers
Samuel Johnson
Oliver Wendell
  Holmes, Sr.
Rupert Brooke
Henry Miller
Marcel Proust
Anaïs Nin
Leo Buscaglia
Voltaire
Morrie Schwartz

Erich Fromm
Benjamin Disraeli
Louisa May Alcott
W. H. Auden
W. Somerset Maugham
Robert Louis
  Stevenson
Albert Schweitzer
Jimi Hendrix
Emily Dickinson
Erich Fromm
Henry Van Dyke
Thomas Carlyle
George Sand
Fred Rogers
Talmud
William Shakespeare
Tom Bodett
Mary Oliver
Thomas Mann
Thomas à Kempis
Carl Sandburg
Anonymous

Johann Wolfgang von
  Goethe
Cesare Pavese
Gerald Jampolsky
Christopher Morley
Elizabeth Barrett
  Browning
Jeanne Moreau
L. Frank Baum
Douglas Jerrold

eLeveN:
tRue Love

François de la
  Rochefoucauld
Honoré de Balzac
Margery Williams
John Donne
Henry Van Dyke
William Shakespeare
Jennifer Aniston
Leo Buscaglia
William Shakespeare

Jim Bishop
Anonymous
Robin St. John
Lao Tzu
Dick Sutphen
Margaret Atwood
Garrison Keillor
Victor Hugo
William Shakespeare
William Goldman
Mark Twain
Sir Walter Scott
David Viscott
Erica Jong
Helen Keller
Elizabeth Barrett
  Browning
Helen Hayes
Leo Buscaglia
Kahlil Gibran
Anonymous
Virgil
Antoine de Saint-Exupéry

Acknowledgments

I am indebted to the following people for their love, support, and creative talents in the making of this book. To my Random House publisher and lifelong friend (and fellow Camp White Swan leader), Sheryl Stebbins, and my editor, Helena Santini, lovingly referred to as "Command Central," thank you both so much for getting this book off and running. To Ian Jackman, my rock and stabling force, I don't even know where to begin to thank you for your editorial knowledge, talent, and calming influence. I am so grateful that you shared your gift with me and our readers. Thank you to my friends who assisted me with suggestions, patient ears, and downright bolstering: Millard Humphreys, Bob Koehler, Ken Hilf, and Larry Brehl. A big thank you goes to my dear friend, Darlene Loebig, who helped me troll the local bookstore for a prized quote or two along with patiently listening to the continuing "Aronson Chronicles." Dar, just you being there helped me more than words can say. I am so grateful to Diane Gloor and

Roberta Eckman in the Volunteer Office of the University of Pittsburgh Medical Center/Passavant Hospital, along with my fellow volunteers who continue to be my favorite cheering section as they filled my empty chair while I worked on this book. To Barb Wyllie, my "Bestest," you are a true example of love in everything you do. Thank you for sharing it with me as well as that shoulder. I'll find that mirror someday, I promise. And finally, to my husband, Tod, thank you for your continued love and understanding and for being my number-one cheerleader with all my endeavors. I am truly blessed with you as my loving spouse. Now, it's my turn to keep the bed warm for you!